NO-FAIL MEETINGS

Also by Michael Hyatt

Your Best Year Ever

Platform: Get Noticed in a Noisy World

Living Forward
(with Daniel Harkavy)

NO-FAIL
MEETINGS

5 Steps to Orchestrate Productive Meetings
(and Avoid All the Rest)

MICHAEL HYATT

Michael Hyatt & Company
Franklin, Tennessee

Published by Michael Hyatt & Company
MichaelHyatt.com

Bulk orders for your team? Email sales@michaelhyatt.com.

ISBN: 1-978-17321896-3-8

Printed in the United States of America

CONTENTS

WHY MEETINGS FAIL

Earlier this week I attended an incredibly productive meeting. It was long, but we accomplished what we set out to do. We stayed on point, had great discussion, made significant decisions, and knew exactly what was expected of us afterward. Everyone left feeling like it was an excellent use of our time—and, believe it or not, we all had fun.

These days, this kind of meeting is the norm for me. But that hasn't always been the case. Throughout my career, I've sat in thousands of meetings. Some of them were good. Many weren't. In fact, I'd say the majority of meetings I've sat through over the past forty years were far less productive than they could have been. Some have been downright awful. I can't be alone in that experience.

We meet more now than ever before. One report found American businesses hold more than three billion meetings per year and eleven million meetings per day. That's a lot of meetings, so it's good they at least contribute to our success, right? Wrong. In fact, meetings may be doing your business more harm than good. Recent studies have shown the unbelievable downside of American meeting culture. In some cases, ineffective meetings are ruining longstanding companies and ending executive careers.

I read an NPR story a while back that put the dangers of bad meetings front and center. Toy manufacturing giant Mattel had fired their CEO, Bryan Stockton. The company struggled for years to keep up with Web-based games and digital competition, and their future looked bleak. But that wasn't Mattel's only problem. "Stockton himself said last year that Mattel lacked an innovative culture and blamed it in part on something specific: bad meetings," NPR's Yuki Noguchi reported in 2015. Even Barbie, Ken, and Thomas the Tank Engine hate corporate meeting culture.

It's not just time spent sitting *in* bad meetings. The drain on time and resources starts well before the scheduled meeting time. The average worker spends nine hours sitting in—or getting ready for—meetings, according to a survey by project management company Clarizen. In fact, six in ten workers say preparing for a simple status meeting takes longer than the meeting itself. "[It's] not just marathon meetings, but meetings that are done to prepare for meetings, and meetings that are done to prepare for meetings to prepare for meetings," business consultant Al Pittampalli told Noguchi. "It's a waste of time—it's what I call a weapon of mass interruption."

Weapon is an appropriate term, because bad meetings are practically killing us. The Clarizen survey found that 46 percent of people would rather do an unpleasant activity like wait in line at the DMV or get a root canal than to sit in a status meeting.

Meetings not only destroy our workplace productivity, efficiency, and satisfaction; they also damage our profitability. TED designer Emily Pidgeon summarized findings on the economic impact of terrible meetings. American companies waste a horrifying $37 billion a year on meetings. A single Fortune 500 company can expect annual losses in excess of $75 million on bad meetings.

Time, perhaps our most valuable resource, takes an even bigger hit than our bottom line. Most employees attend an average of sixty-two meetings per month. Executives spend 40 to 50 percent of their work time—an average of twenty-three hours per week—sitting in meetings. Even worse, almost 34 percent of an executive's total meeting time is spent in meetings that are unnecessary and poorly run. That equates to more than two months per year down the drain. Something's got to change.

INTERRUPTED BY MEETINGS

Meetings have become interruptions, and the interruptions begin before the meeting ever does. See if this sounds familiar: It's mid-morning, and you're working on something important in your office. The day had a bumpy start, but now you're in the flow. You have quieted all the distractions that tried to steal your attention, and you've been laser-focused on a critical task for a half-hour. You're *finally* making progress. And then—

Ding! Your cell phone chimes out a meeting reminder. You need to be in the conference room in fifteen minutes. Why? Weekly status meeting. What do you have to report? Nothing. What impact will the meeting have on your personal projects? None. Who would miss you if you weren't there? No one. How long will it last? It's scheduled for an hour, but these things usually run at least ten minutes late—and that's assuming they start on time, which they rarely do. So, what do you do?

You stop working. You've already lost your focus. Your momentum on your critical project has hit a wall. You stand up, walk over to the coffee pot in the break room, fill your enormous mug (you're going to need it for this meeting), and trudge toward the conference room, otherwise known as the place where productivity goes to die. They might as well placard the doorway: "Abandon hope, all ye who enter here."

It gets worse. You have a team lunch after this, followed by more meetings in the afternoon. You sigh and accept that you've already accomplished everything of significance you'll be able to do. Your productive day is practically over after only thirty minutes of real work.

How does this happen? Why do we allow meetings to steal so much time, money, and attention? Because of a common but dangerous misconception. We believe the lie that meetings are where work takes place. But here's the truth: Most meetings aren't work. They make us *think* we're working, but most of the time we're not, unless the meeting is led especially well (something I'll show you how to do in this book).

At best, poorly run meetings give us the chance to *talk* about work; we spend an hour discussing work we'll do later. Then, we leave that meeting and head into another one where we do the same thing. Rinse and repeat. By the end of the day, we might have spent six hours *talking* about work and no time actually *doing* any.

Later, when we finally get home, we say hello to the family, eat dinner, and then—you guessed it—retreat to our home offices to get our work done. Wouldn't it be nice if we could have enough time in the workday to actually work instead of having to bring it home? I'm certain you can. But only if you transform the way you do meetings.

Yes, meetings can drain, distract, and drag us away from truly important work. They can waste time and money and leave us exhausted without providing real progress on our high-leverage goals. They look like work, act like work, and feel like work—but they usually aren't work. Meetings are monsters masquerading as productivity. But here's the good news: We can do this better.

STOP FAILING AT MEETINGS

Leaders often put meetings on the calendar with no real

thought, and then they walk into meetings with no preparation. They haphazardly throw a group of people into a room, at least some of whom aren't even needed for the discussion at hand. They don't follow an agenda, don't maximize virtual meeting technology, don't assign takeaway actions, and don't hold people accountable later for what they spent an hour or more discussing. At the end of the day, "traditional" meetings go nowhere. They fail.

They fail their purpose. They fail the hopes of the people who schedule them. They fail the teams who depend on their outcomes. And that's a shame because meetings hold enormous potential for streamlining our projects, increasing our profits, transforming our work culture, and connecting our teams. They provide opportunities for collaboration, creativity, and connection. And, believe it or not, meetings can be fun!

They don't have to fail. That's a choice.

This little book will show you how to run meetings that work. It'll even show you how to eliminate the rest. When you remove the bad meetings and improve the rest, you'll change your organization's entire attitude about working together. You'll create an atmosphere of cooperation and collaboration, giving your team the chance to work together in ways that produce powerful results while still being enjoyable for every team member.

Plus, you'll remove the dread that many people associate with meetings in a corporate culture and maximize everyone's time and personal productivity. In short, you'll be a hero!

5 STEPS TO NO FAIL MEETINGS

The path to transforming your company's meeting culture starts with five simple steps that make up the heart of the No Fail Meetings system:

1. *Decide* if the meeting is even necessary and, if so, what type and format it should be.

2. *Schedule* the right *people* at the right *time* for the right *length* in the right *location*.

3. *Prepare* a results-driven agenda.

4. *Meet* and engage in a powerful, productive conversation that moves the needle for your business and projects.

5. *Follow up* by reviewing your meeting notes, completing your assigned tasks, and holding others accountable for theirs.

What if you decided to never host another low-leverage, ineffectual meeting? What if you put a stake in the ground and said *this* is the year your meetings become effective, helpful and—dare I say—*awesome*? It's possible, and it begins by making some key decisions about your meeting.

STEP 1

DECIDE

Syncing up your team for success takes three things: contact, communication, and connection. A good meeting covers all three bases. First, it gives you meaningful *contact* with your team members. It reminds them that you're a real person, not some distant figure in a far-off corner office. Second, meetings keep you in regular *communication* with your team. You can't keep everyone aligned if they never see or hear from you. The more you speak into their work, the more you'll be able to trust the outcomes. Third, meetings give you a *connection* with the people you're working with. And that's where trust and real cooperation is born.

If your team is going to achieve major goals, you need to be able to plan, coordinate, and tackle problems together. Meetings have the power to focus thinking, create alignment, force decisions, and drive results. In fact, 97 percent of employees consider that kind of collaboration essential for doing their best work, according to Joanne Cleaver in an article for *Business Researcher*.

We don't want to abolish all meetings. Instead, we have to train our teams to lead great meetings. That begins with making some key decisions about the meeting itself, and the best way to do that is by answering five filtering questions:

❶ Is this meeting necessary?

❷ Are you sure you're necessary?

③ Who else should be involved?

④ What type of meeting do you want?

⑤ What's the right format?

These are useful for both evaluating outgoing and incoming meeting requests. Let's take them in order.

IS THIS MEETING NECESSARY?

The first decision you need to make—and a step we too often skip—is to simply ask if a meeting is necessary. As a rule, we're too quick to meet. When a question or problem pops up, it is easier to say, "Let's set up a meeting" than it is to spend a few brain cycles in the moment to solve the problem. In the process, we turn what might have been a ten-minute chat today into an hour-long meeting tomorrow.

This doesn't mean you should allow yourself to get distracted by pop-up questions all day. If you're focused on one task, you should stay focused on that task; that's the essence of productivity. However, if you can avoid a meeting by simply setting aside a few minutes later in the day to process a problem you need to solve or a question you need to answer, then do it. There's no reason for a group of people to gather in a conference room. By punting to a meeting, you're (a) outsourcing your thinking, (b) enlisting others in your procrastination, or (c) both.

Let's say you land on a solution. You might be tempted to get everyone in a room and announce your decision. Resist the impulse. You can usually get by updating people via email, Slack, or your project management system. The only thing worse than having a roomful of people sit around watching someone make a decision is calling that group back to tell them what the decision was. That's called a "status meeting," and people hate those.

We think we're boosting productivity by bringing everyone together to distribute information, but we're doing the reverse. Forty-five percent of all meetings are about status updates or disseminating information, according to Cleaver. These kind of meetings cost the average American worker a quarter of their workweek, and one third of those stuck attending consider them a complete waste of time, according to the Clarizen survey already mentioned.

That's fair. We slow people down to bring them up to speed, spending hours a week in meetings for updates that would take minutes to read in Slack, Asana, or whatever communication or project-management solution you're using. Meanwhile, says Cleaver, only 5 percent of all meetings facilitate brainstorming or other creative functions—in other words, the kinds of meetings people actually enjoy.

If you're a leader, it's your responsibility to decide if a meeting is necessary. Your team has entrusted you with their time. Make it a priority to steward those hours by carefully examining the purpose of each meeting request and ensuring it's the single best way to accomplish the goal at hand. At MH&Co, we only schedule meetings if the purpose of the meeting is high-leverage. Typically, that refers to people and profit. If a meeting is high-leverage, it deals with the most important people we serve (our staff, clients, and customers) or our profit (how to increase, protect, spend, or manage it). Your leverage points might look different, depending on your priorities. Regardless, figure out what *high-leverage* means for you and then make sure your meetings support those goals.

Sometimes it's easier to spot low-leverage meetings. The following questions can help point those out. Ask these when evaluating existing or potential meetings:

- Do we need a meeting at all? Could I, as the leader, simply make a call about the issue at hand instead of roping in other people and belaboring the decision?

- If this is a recurring meeting established more than six months ago, is it still beneficial? Should it be repurposed? Could it be canceled?

- Could we accomplish our desired outcome just as easily a different way, such as an email exchange or a phone call?

- Could a subset of the group meet or talk offline and still achieve the meeting purpose?

If you review these questions and decide that a meeting is necessary, it's your job to make it as productive as possible. The rest of *No-Fail Meetings* will help you with that.

ARE YOU SURE YOU'RE NECESSARY?

If you're like most people, you get a steady stream of meeting invitations all day, every day. You need to decide about these as well.

Back when I was the CEO of a large publishing house, I had two full-time assistants. One of them was wholly devoted to managing my calendar. She spent forty hours a week dealing with a never-ending avalanche of invitations and meeting requests. I blindly accepted those requests for far too long. As a recovering people-pleaser, my default position when someone asked for my time was to say yes. I assumed if they asked, then my presence must be necessary. Bad assumption.

I was guilty then—and I bet some of you are now—of what David Grady calls "Mindless Accept Syndrome" or MAS. "The primary symptom of Mindless Accept Syndrome is just accepting a meeting invitation the minute it pops up in your calendar," he said in a helpful TED

Talk. "It's an involuntary reflex: ding, click, bam—it's on your calendar."

But that's a big mistake. Accepting meeting requests is like swiping a debit card. You can only do it so long before you run out of resources—in this case, time, the most valuable resource of all. It doesn't matter how worthy a use of your time might seem; you only have so much. And just like your debit card, nobody knows the balance but you. There's no cost in asking for your time, but plenty of cost in your giving it away.

You'll always have more opportunities than time. Accepting too many meetings leaves you overcommitted and prevents you from doing your best work. If you give your time away to anyone who asks, you'll never have enough left to accomplish your most meaningful work—the work *only you* can do. Before hitting "accept" on your next meeting request, ask:

- Is this meeting important?
- Is it important for me?
- Can I afford the time given my other priorities?
- Could someone else take my place?
- Is there another way this request could be handled?

Sometimes it's difficult to decipher from a request

if a meeting is necessary or not. The questions we've already posed above can help. Another trick is to reframe: Instead of asking whether *the meeting* is necessary, ask whether *you* are necessary for the meeting. If you're not, don't be scared to say no. And always feel free to push back on the request for more information.

If you don't put boundaries in place, you'll allow other people to dictate your entire schedule. And you're not helping anyone by stretching yourself too thin. If your default invitation response is *yes*, it's time to flip the switch. Challenge yourself to say *no* to everything unless there's a compelling reason to say *yes*. That may mean having to retrain your team to send better, more informative meeting requests. We'll cover that in Step 2.

WHO ELSE SHOULD BE INVOLVED?

We are usually too quick to overlook the hard costs of meetings. Try this: Pick an upcoming meeting on your calendar—preferably one that's an hour in length and one that you scheduled. Now, run through the list of people you invited to the meeting. Whether you know their real salaries or not, try to estimate the hourly pay of each team member on the list. From there, add up the payroll that is represented in the meeting, including your own time and the time of any other executives in the room. You may be shocked by what you find.

That single, hour-long "quick check-in" meeting could cost you thousands of dollars. If this is a weekly meeting, multiply it by 52 to see the yearly impact this routine meeting has to your bottom line. As we've already seen, a Fortune 500 company loses up to $75 million per year due to poor meetings. Emily Pidgeon says a single meeting between executives may cost the typical company more than $1,000 in salary costs alone.

And don't forget that you aren't only losing money; you're also losing time. If ten people attend that weekly meeting, you're losing ten hours of company time every week—or 520 hours every year. If you aren't getting that much value out of the meeting, then it shouldn't be on your calendar (or anyone else's).

So, how do you decide how many people to invite? Part of counting the cost involves counting heads. And that's useful for another reason. If an informational meeting is required, a large group may be appropriate. However, getting several busy people together in one room at the same time can become a scheduling nightmare. It costs you not only the expense of the people hours during the meeting, but also the expense of several assistants figuring out when and where to schedule the meeting.

If the informational meeting turns into a discussion, you're sunk. Getting a large group of people aligned around one conversation to drive one decision is next to impossible. Instead, if the purpose of the meeting is to debate or discuss, I recommend inviting as few people as necessary. Small groups are nimbler, can assemble more quickly, and make decisions faster.

Once the decision is made, you can communicate the outcome to the rest of the team in a quick, informational meeting or, better yet, through an email or project management status update. The key here is that more people create more complexity, and you want to challenge and/or eliminate anything that gets in the way of staying quick and nimble.

WHAT TYPE OF MEETING DO YOU WANT?

If you're sure the meeting is necessary, the next step is to decide what *type* of meeting will work best. Most meetings tend to fall within two main types: routine meetings and one-offs. If you spend any time at all in meetings, these two types will be instantly familiar.

Routine meetings recur on some set schedule: daily, weekly, monthly, quarterly, and even annually. You can see these coming, they're a natural part of your routine, and they should be easy to create agendas for. Because of their regularity, these can be the most efficient of all meetings. I lead a weekly MH&Co status update that includes the whole staff. It's not only worth the cost (per above), but it keeps attendees aligned around our goals, attuned to our progress, and aware what top-level activity each department is prioritizing for the week.

That works for us. But many organizations go astray with routine meetings. How? Usually because meeting organizers don't ensure the purpose is relevant to the participants. Often routine meetings like these exist because "that's how we've always done it." While there can be a lot of value in recurring meetings, it's time to reevaluate each one to see whether or not it's really necessary.

There are three primary purposes for routine meetings:

First, *goal tracking.* This keeps your department and company-wide goals front and center. It helps you track how everyone is contributing to the overall goals of the company and make sure everyone is moving in the right direction.

Second, *priority reviews.* Routine meetings also give you a recurring opportunity to review each team and team member's priorities. You can stay up-to-date on what they're working on and make sure those efforts are all working toward the overall company goals.

Third, *troubleshooting.* Most routine meetings include general updates, challenges, and ideas. This gives everyone in attendance—especially leaders—the chance to offer solutions and make decisions on the spot. This can be especially helpful if the leader's time is short and the team depends on these meetings for critical facetime with decision-makers.

Routine meetings are often internal, meaning these are usually for employees of the company. You could occasionally have routine meetings with external people, such as outside contractors or vendors, but generally, routine meetings are team-time. That means you can customize these meetings with your unique corporate culture, internal vocabulary, and inside jokes. Familiarity is great here, but it can easily turn into stagnation if you're not careful. The antidote for this is a bulletproof agenda, which we will cover in Step 3.

I've compiled a list of the different routine meetings my company regularly holds, which you can review in the Resources section at the back of this book. You'll see things like the Daily Executive Assistant Check-in meeting that many of my leaders have with their admins, the Weekly Department Huddle that our individual departments use to review their specific goals and priorities, and the Monthly Leadership Team Meeting that keeps our leaders connected. This list works well for us, but your mileage may vary. You'll need to see what works best for you and your team. Feel free to copy, customize, or cut our list as needed, if it helps you.

One-offs are nonrecurring meetings. These are usually project-related and are a mix of internal and external people. Because these meeting topics and participants vary, it can be hard to create agenda templates to guide the discussion. This can easily result in a meandering meeting if you aren't careful. So, when calling a one-off meeting, be sure to devote enough time to prepare properly. A standardized meeting template can help. I cover that in Step 3.

WHAT'S THE RIGHT FORMAT?

Assuming you've decided a meeting is necessary, who should be involved, and what type of meeting it should be, you now must decide on the format. You've got some options here—either meet in-person or virtually via a video conferencing solution.

If you work in a "traditional" office environment, most of your meetings are probably face-to-face, sitting around a big conference table or huddled in someone's office. These in-person meetings give you enormous opportunity to build relationships with your team members and connect on a personal level. Sharing a workspace and being able to gather quickly for impromptu meetings develops friendship and trust, and that can translate into better, more efficient work. That level of personal interaction can make a huge impact on your meetings, as half of all employees say face-to-face meetings are *very* effective, according to Cleaver, and 84 percent say they're at least *somewhat* effective compared to virtual meetings.

While in-person meetings may have an edge in building relationships, technology has come a long way over the past decade in virtual meeting solutions. As of 2018, I'd say 80 percent of my company's meetings are virtual. Most of our team works remotely, and the video conferencing app Zoom works great for daily, weekly, and one-off meetings.

What about old-timey conference calls? I'm not a fan. You can't read people's expressions and body language, you can't instantly share resources or visuals during the call, you can't easily record the meeting audio, and you can never be sure if the quiet person on the other end of the line has somehow been disconnected or just fallen asleep.

Quality video conferencing solves all of that. It puts your team right in front of you anytime, no matter where on earth they are. The biggest danger is poor technology or connectivity problems. You'll want to pick a top-quality service—as we've found Zoom to be—and make sure you've got reliable high-speed Internet. There will still be glitches from time to time, but I've only had a handful of Zoom meetings fail due to technology problems over the past few years. The upside of virtual meetings has far outweighed the negatives for us, as it has allowed our team the freedom and flexibility to work from anywhere.

Importantly, the No-Fail Meetings system works in either meeting format. I don't believe one is inherently better than the other. It comes down to how well the meeting is organized, how it's led, and the outcome you're after. If we can build our team, grow our initiatives, and hit our goals with virtual meetings, we'll do that. If we need to bring everyone together to hash out an issue in person, we'll do that. Every organization—every meeting—is different, so the best option is to get familiar with the different solutions and pick the best one for each meeting.

Now that you've decided on your meeting, it's time to get it on the calendar. And, as you'll find out in Step 2, the simple matter of scheduling isn't simple at all.

STEP 2

SCHEDULE

Too many people approach scheduling like a game of Battleship. When they need to set up a one-off meeting, for example, they open the calendar, find an opening, and drop a meeting bomb. Of course, they're also hoping everyone else's calendars look just like theirs, so their availability syncs up—but that's almost never the case.

As a result, you or your assistant can literally spend hours trying to coordinate with other people, teams, and admins to find a day and time that works for everyone. There's no rhyme or reason; it's all about plugging holes in a dozen different calendars.

Depending on who's needed in the meeting, it could be weeks before you're able to meet about something, and the meeting that's so important to you will almost certainly become an unwelcome interruption to the people you're trying to connect with. Let's be honest: You know you feel that way about many of the meetings you're invited to. It only stands to reason that everyone else feels the same way when they get a meeting invitation from you.

There may not be a way to completely eliminate the hassle from scheduling meetings, but my team has found a way to cut out 90 percent of it. How? By focusing on three key factors of scheduling: *when*, *where*, and *how*.

WHEN TO MEET?

There are two aspects of when: date and time. Let's look at the first.

Date. In my productivity course, *Free to Focus*, I teach a system called the Ideal Week. It's a way of batching your activity so you can focus on your most important work. You can use the Ideal Week system on your own, but implementing this system across your whole team or company yields even more transformative results.

Here's how it works in a nutshell. Print out a blank weekly calendar. You want to start with zero appointments or commitments. You're going to organize your Ideal Week by three categories of tasks or activity: Front Stage, Back Stage, and Off Stage.

Front Stage. These tasks represent your most important work. These are the things you were hired to do. If you're a writer, this is time you spend writing. If you're a litigator, this is the time you spend arguing in court. If you're a graphic designer, this is the time you spend designing. Here's an easy heuristic to use: If it appears on your annual review, it's probably a Front Stage activity.

Back Stage. These are the tasks that enable you to do your Front Stage work. This could include things like doing research, updating quarterly budgets for your area, filing expense reports, and meeting with team members. In fact, most of the meetings we have on any given day are Back Stage work. They enable us to accomplish our Front Stage tasks, but we weren't specifically hired to sit in meetings. That's the difference.

Off Stage. This is the time when we're not at work, not doing work, not thinking about work, not even reading about work. As I argue in *Free to Focus*, going Off Stage is essential for personal rejuvenation. Let's assume nights and weekends are Off Stage and therefore off limits for work-related meetings—except, say, the occasional client dinner.

The most effective way to handle meetings are to batch them along with other Back Stage activities and keep as much uninterrupted Front Stage time as possible. I advise dedicating entire days to both Back Stage and Front Stage work. For me, Saturday and Sunday are always Off Stage, Monday and Friday are Back Stage, and Tuesday through Thursday are Front Stage. That designation alone gives me some clarity around when I should schedule meetings. I have relegated meetings to my Back Stage time, so I try to schedule all my meetings on Mondays and Fridays. Meetings don't feel like interruptions because I don't plan any Front Stage work on those days. I'm never pulled away from my most important work to run off to a meeting.

I even take this organization one step further and, as much as possible, devote Mondays to *internal* meetings (with my team members) and Fridays to *external* meetings (with people outside my organization). This makes it easy for my assistant to know my availability, and it sets the right expectation for my team members if they need a meeting with me.

We've implemented a version of the Ideal Week for our whole company. How? We schedule times when our entire team does not have any meetings. That is, we block off time each week (Thursdays) when no one is allowed to schedule any meeting with anyone. That may seem counterintuitive, but it ensures everyone gets uninterrupted blocks of time for their most important tasks. We know that we show up as our best selves *for* meetings when we haven't already spent all our working hours *in* meetings. Because we're aligned on an overarching schedule, it's easier to preserve time for what Georgetown computer science professor Cal Newport calls "deep work" on Front Stage days.

If you want to get the best out of your meeting time, and if you have the authority or top-level buy-in to do it, put some hard boundaries around when meetings are allowed. It has worked wonders for not only our meeting culture, but also team morale and general productivity.

What if you can't do this across the board? I recommend creating your Ideal Week and letting it guide your meeting schedule regardless, whether it's setting or accepting meetings. Don't suggest meeting times that fall on your Front Stage days, and as far as it's within your power don't accept meetings on those days, either. If you have to accept some, try to group them at the top or bottom of the day so they don't break up your focus in the middle of the day.

To protect your calendar from everyone else, set appointments with yourself. In their book *Rework*, Jason Fried and David Heinemeier Hansson call this time in the Alone Zone. Let your calendar say no for you; schedule a meeting with yourself and flag the time as busy or unavailable.

One final challenge warrants our attention. How do you get several people with independent schedules into one room (real or virtual) at the same time? One answer is to use an administrative assistant. In fact, if you employ an administrative assistant, you should never schedule your own meetings. First, you're not that good at it, are you? Second, it's not the best use of your time. But what if you don't have an admin? One solution I've used and love is Calendly, this is especially helpful if you're trying to meet with people outside your organization. Calendly lets you set your available times; meeting attendees can then find what works best for them from the available time slots.

That's the first consideration, date. What about time?

Time. Few things will impact a productive workday like losing an hour on a discussion that should have taken ten minutes. The problem is that we are not intentional enough when we schedule time for a meeting. We act like the default meeting length is thirty minutes or an hour—that costs us hours in lost productivity every week.

Why do we allow a short conversation to stretch into an hour of aimless discussion? It's because of Parkinson's Law: *Work expands to the time allotted to it.* If you schedule two hours for a meeting, guess what? The meeting will take two hours—whether it really *deserves* two hours or not. Once I understood the impact of Parkinson's Law on my work and meetings, I started to apply what my team calls Hyatt's Corollary: *Work shrinks to the time allotted to it.* So, if you want your meetings to take up less of your time, you need to *schedule* them for less of your time. That means shorter meetings.

Taking a cue from psychological research that shows our average attention span is about eighteen minutes, the most effective leaders set meetings for as brief a time as fifteen or even ten minutes, according to *Fast Company* writer Kevan Lee. Sometimes, these short meetings need more time and require a follow-up meeting. Usually, however, everyone in the meeting stays aware of the compressed time frame and keeps the meeting on point, arriving at decisions faster and easier than they ever thought possible. That's Parkinson's Law (and Hyatt's Corollary) in action.

Of course, whether you schedule your meeting for

ten minutes or two hours, you need to honor the time commitment you've asked of the other participants. That means starting and ending the meeting on time. When you start late, you inadvertently penalize the punctual and reward the tardy. This makes the problem *worse*, not better. We're literally training people to arrive late because they know nothing significant happens until well after the start time.

Likewise, finishing late frustrates the participants because they all have other things to get to. Meetings that run late cascade into other meetings that then must also start late. One poorly-led meeting first thing in the morning can literally throw your entire day off track, and you'll be scrambling to make up the lost time all day. Instead, we must be disciplined about starting and finishing on time. It's amazing how much you can cover if you know the clock is ticking.

WHERE TO MEET?

Once you figure out when and how long to meet, you can identify the ideal location for your meeting. Many companies rely on the traditional on-site conference room for routine and one-off meetings, and that can work fine. However, as teams get more diverse and remote working continues to expand across our companies, I think it's time to start thinking outside the box.

For example, my company uses a variety of locations for meetings. On any given week, you can find our team members meeting virtually over Zoom or Slack (via video call) or in person at one of our co-working spaces; someone's home office or dining room table, and at our favorite restaurants and coffee shops. One of our executives conducts several meetings a week by phone as he walks.

Virtual meetings give each participant the freedom to meet from anywhere. I suggest bringing that same philosophy to the in-person meetings you host. Don't lock yourself down to the same locations for all your meetings. Instead, inject some variety and fun into your meetings.

Shaking things up by breaking the traditional corporate mold will unlock a surprising amount of creativity, productivity, and inspiration in your meeting—and all these things will make not only the conversation but also the quality of the work ten times better. The location you select just needs to meet the requirements of the specific meeting and include a dash of inspiration.

Does the meeting require a lot of note-taking, printed materials, and viewing documents together? If so, a restaurant, coffee shop, or park probably isn't your best bet. You'll need a space with comfortable chairs, tables, and a way to display the presentation. If it doesn't require much note-taking or document review, the information being discussed isn't especially confidential, and you're looking to really connect with the person you're meeting with, a more casual meeting at a coffee shop or restaurant will work well.

Maybe you want the meeting to be more personally connective and away from the traditional office setting, but you need it to be someplace quiet for a confidential conversation. Consider booking a private room at a restaurant, hosting the meeting at a team member's home, or using a private space in your office/co-working space. You want to be free to talk without feeling like you need to whisper.

Is this a brainstorming meeting where ideation and creativity are important? If so, consider renting a house or condo for the day near your office. This gets your team out of the ordinary meeting spaces, provides privacy, and gives them comfortable couches and plenty of room to spread out. We've hosted these kinds of meetings in vacation rentals within walking distance to great restaurants and in rental cottages in the woods for extended meetings and retreats.

Wherever you choose to meet, just remember that creative meetings often require creative meeting spaces. We'll talk more about how to set up your meeting space in Step 3.

HOW TO INVITE PARTICIPANTS?

In Step 1, we discussed the invitation's *who* (you and

others). In Step 2, we've so far discussed the invite's *when* and *where*. What about the *how*? Many of us schedule meetings with nothing more than a haphazard meeting title and time. That's not enough.

As I mentioned in Step 1, for years I suffered from what David Grady calls "Mindless Accept Syndrome," blindly accepting whatever invitation someone sent me. Sometimes my MAS came from a lack of intentionality. Other times it came from a fear of saying no. Either way, it prevented me from calling out what was glaringly obvious: most meeting invitations are terrible! They presume the attendee has nothing better to do, so they don't bother providing enough data to make an informed decision about attending. But our time is important; we can't afford to waste it. As Seneca said, spending our time is "the one thing in which it is right to be stingy." So, what's the solution? Training people how to send better meeting invitations.

Grady suggests two simple steps that he calls his *No MAS!* response. First, whenever you receive an invitation with insufficient information about the meeting, respond as *tentative*. Then, reach out to the meeting organizer. Tell them you want to help but you need more information before you can commit your time. Make them articulate the goal of the meeting and explain how you can add to the discussion, and then decide whether to change your *tentative* response to *accept*—or *decline*.

By doing this consistently as you receive meeting invitations, you'll re-train those around you to send complete, detailed meeting requests.

This goes both ways, of course. You owe the same treatment to others when you schedule a meeting. Remember, you're asking people to give up their time to help you solve a problem, so extend them the courtesy of communicating up front what the meeting is about, how long it will take, what the goal of the meeting is, and how they can help achieve that goal. If you can't be bothered to give them that much information, then they shouldn't have to bother attending your meeting.

I recovered from a near-terminal case of MAS by refusing to accept any meeting that did not come with an agenda. That had the benefit of ensuring the meeting request was thought-out and that the sender had some skin in the game. What do I mean? It's no cost to send a slapdash meeting request, but it takes some time to draft a workable agenda. And that takes us to Step 3.

At this point, you've made several key decisions about the *who*, *what*, *when*, *where*, and at least some of the *how*. But don't jump the gun. If you meet before the next step, you'll be doing everyone in the room a great disservice—not to mention wasting their time. Before the meeting starts, you must plan the meeting. That's what we'll cover next.

PREPARE

believe most of the bad meetings you've attended in the past can be traced back to one missing piece: preparation. Too often, leaders or project managers pull groups of team members into conference rooms without taking any time to figure out what they'll do when they get there. Or they may get the group together hoping that the team itself can figure out what they should discuss during the meeting. How often does that actually happen?

Wharton management professor Nancy Rothbard thinks the problem is that we're already so overbooked with meetings it cuts into our ability to think about the issue beforehand. "There are so many demands on us that leaders are scheduling meetings to get people engaged in the problem at hand," she says in an article for *Knowledge@Wharton*. "I think people call meetings so they can have people's mindshare, when it might have been more efficient to work through a problem independently."

You should never call a meeting if you could do the work better—and more efficiently—on your own. You'll only know if that's possible, though, if you think through the meeting ahead of time. You called the meeting; it's your responsibility to prepare for it. That means writing out a rock-solid, well-thought-out meeting agenda and preparing a meeting space customized for your purpose and attendees.

PREPARE THE PERFECT AGENDA

People go wrong with agendas in two different ways: too little or too much. Either they dash off something far too broad (and thus vague) for the scope of the meeting, or they create an overcomplicated, cumbersome, time-gobbling task they hate (and then frequently skip). Both outcomes lead to failure. I've got something better.

The agenda template we use at MH&Co is only one sheet, but it creates clarity for the meeting leader and for each attendee. You can find a copy of the meeting template in the Resources section at the end of this book. We'll walk through each part of it here. Feel free to copy this template and use it for your meetings.

The template is broken down into three sections: basic info, purpose, and program. Let's look at each.

Basic information. Every meeting agenda should feature these "what, when, and who" details up top:

① Meeting title

② Date and time

③ Participants

④ Meeting leader

⑤ Meeting facilitator

Every meeting needs a title just like every book needs one and for the same reason: it informs people about the contents. Date and time are obvious, as are participants. But what of the meeting leader and facilitator?

The meeting leader is a strategic role, whereas the facilitator handles meeting processes. The leader sets the purpose of the meeting and owns the results. They drive the meeting and lead the discussion. The facilitator prepares the agenda with input from the leader, distributes the agenda, keeps time, takes and distributes notes, and follows up on any action items. The facilitator might be an administrative assistant or someone else who agrees to serve the role; the latter is an important option on smaller teams. It's hard for a leader to play both roles.

Recording this information might seem like an obvious step, but it's funny how many people don't bother. You may remember who was in a meeting last week, but if you're looking back on meeting notes from a year or two ago, you'll be glad you took the time to write everyone's name down on the agenda. Besides, as we'll see, every meeting should end with task assignments for the participants. Keeping the list of attendees will ensure you know whom to follow up with later.

Meeting purpose. Next, record the meeting purpose. This is where you clarify *why* the team is meeting. At the start of the process, you decided that a meeting was necessary. Now, it's time to articulate that necessity into a specific purpose or goal for the meeting.

If you can't succinctly state what you hope to accomplish in the meeting, you should take it off the calendar. Nobody wants to take time out of their busy day to sit in a room and watch you try to define the meeting goals in real-time. Instead, clearly state the meeting purpose on the agenda, followed by two or three specific results you hope to accomplish.

Specific is the key word here. "Talk about Q3 and Q4" is not a good meeting purpose. Instead, you might say, "The purpose is to review the company's Q3 financial results and brainstorm three new actions to close the gap in Q4." This is a critical step. Whatever you write in this section will ultimately determine if your meeting is a success or a failure. Your stated purpose is the measuring stick, so put some thought into this.

Program. Don't think of this as a list of bullet points or questions you want to cover. Instead, think of the program like a personal budget. Time is your currency, and you want to spend it wisely. Our program template is broken down into four main sections. These are the areas we cover most times we meet:

First, *achievements.* Celebrating milestones and accomplishments sets the tone for a positive meeting. As high-achievers, we often fail to remember this step, so we memorialized it in our agenda. Leaders should take advantage of small moments of encouragement every day; meetings, where your team is already gathered, are a great opportunity—especially in recurring meetings. It's not necessary every time, and don't force it. But don't skip it if it will give you a chance to build your team's spirit.

Second, *expectations*. Misaligned expectations can destroy a meeting before it even gets off the ground. That's why it is so important to devote a few minutes early in the meeting to get everyone on the same page. You can do this by quickly stating the meeting purpose, clarifying the roles (leader and facilitator), and reviewing the agenda. As part of the agenda overview, you should also note how much time is allocated to each point of discussion and remind everyone the facilitator is keeping time. Finally, affirm that the meeting will end on time.

Third, *issues*. Once everyone is on the same page, it's time to discuss the specific issues that brought everyone together. On the MH&Co template, this is indicated by "Meeting Content" fields. Here, you want to clarify exactly what needs to be discussed or presented in the meeting. As you prepare, think through the entire conversation. Ask yourself what needs to happen to make this meeting a success, who needs to report in, what information is missing, and what topics will cause this meeting to fail if you don't cover it. If this is a recurring meeting, you should use this time to review the minutes and action items from the previous meeting. Follow up on tasks that were assigned to others and get status updates from the individual teams. Your meetings should drive actions and decisions, and you want to make sure the previous meeting got the results you wanted. This also holds everyone in the room accountable to the work that comes out of these meetings.

Fourth, *ownership*. For your meeting to produce results, each team member needs to know exactly what's expected after the meeting. Leave a few minutes at the end to have each person (or at least each department leader) share their action items and responsibilities resulting from this meeting. This should be brief and should not cover their entire game plan; they should simply share their next one to three steps to execute on what's been discussed. They should also commit to a time that they'll be able to deliver on these commitments.

This step requires discipline to enforce, because it is so easy to drive a meeting discussion right up to the scheduled end time. Don't do it. Safeguard the final few minutes of the meeting to make sure everyone knows their marching orders. If everyone leaves in a rush to get to their next meeting, they won't be set up with the full ownership they need to produce the results you want. (By the way, the Extra Resources section in the back also provides a template for taking meeting notes that meeting facilitators may find helpful.)

One helpful mnemonic for remembering these

agenda elements is the list of vowels: AEIO (but no U): achievements, expectations, issues, ownership. If you commit to run through this agenda prep, you'll revolutionize your organization's meeting culture. Again, people usually hate meetings because they aren't necessary or the meeting organizer doesn't know what they're doing. By walking through this process, you're eliminating both of those dangers.

And if at any point in this preparation process you realize critical information is missing, the goal of the meeting is unclear, or the meeting purpose can be accomplished *without* a meeting, don't hesitate to cancel. Just do it well ahead of time so your attendees don't waste any time preparing.

PREPARE THE MEETING SPACE

As the meeting organizer, you need to put a little thought into where the meeting will take place and how well the room accommodates the specific needs of the meeting. We covered this a bit in the previous step, and you may have already picked a great meeting location. Regardless of the location you selected, there are a few things you should keep in mind to ensure you're creating an inspiring environment that will encourage discussion, trust, vulnerability, and creativity.

First, the room aesthetics need to be on point.

Whether you're decorating your own office environment, selecting an outside facility, or choosing a restaurant to meet at, remember that beauty helps inspire breakthrough thinking. If this isn't your thing, delegate it to someone on your team or hire someone to help. Even if *you* don't think it matters, others *will*. Do not overlook this point. You can't afford your meeting space to distract or disgust your participants.

Second, natural light is important. Most people forget to consider appropriate lighting when setting up an office space or selecting a place to meet, but nobody wants to work—or have a creative discussion—in a windowless cave. In fact, a global survey of employees found that 75 percent of workers value natural light, but only 56 percent are satisfied with their lighting conditions at work, according to Bob Ford in *Workplace Design*. Consider these words from Christopher Bergland in *Psychology Today*,

> There is a strong relationship between workplace daylight exposure and office workers' sleep, activity, and quality of life . . . Compared to workers in offices without windows, those with windows in the workplace received 173 percent more white light exposure during work hours and slept an average of 46 minutes more per night. Workers without windows reported lower scores than their counterparts on quality of life measures related to physical problems

and vitality. They also had poorer outcomes in measures of overall sleep quality, sleep efficiency, sleep disturbances, and daytime dysfunction.

Staying in the dark or being force-fed fluorescent light all day makes us tired, weak, sad, and stupid! Whenever possible, support your team's productivity by selecting meeting spaces that have great natural light. Consider scheduling breaks to walk outside and get some sunshine during long meetings. You might even hold meetings outside if the weather is nice, as long as your meeting doesn't require presentations or a lot of papers.

Third, comfort is crucial, especially if you're hosting a long meeting. Whenever possible, utilize comfortable chairs and tables that are an appropriate height. Also, select or create a space where there's enough room for people to move during meetings as needed. Give people permission to stand up, walk around, or lean up against walls during the meeting. Sometimes, keeping them locked in a chair is the *worst* thing for keeping their attention. Pacing can be great for thought and processing new ideas.

Fourth, provide nourishment. Our days are often busy, and occasionally, your meeting attendees haven't slowed down long enough to eat anything all day. If you want to keep them engaged, you need to help them stay fueled. Your meeting can be an opportunity for them to have a bite to eat, which could give a much-needed boost to their blood sugar levels. If you're meeting at your office, make sure you have a supply cabinet or kitchen stocked with healthy snacks. If you're meeting offsite, pack a grocery bag of snacks, bottled water, and coffee for your meeting. When appropriate, consider cocktails. Leaders often use touches like this only when trying to impress external customers, clients, or vendors, but our teams deserve our best, too.

Fifth, strive to deliver a "wow experience." This isn't necessary every time, but you can spice up for special meetings by thinking about ways to wow the guests at your meeting. Doing the steps above will already make your meetings better than most, but consider how you could take this to the next level. You could set a small gift on the table for them, or do a drawing for a gift card just to say thank you, present handwritten notes to each attendee to express your gratitude, have fresh flowers on the table, or maybe throw out some office toys and stress balls to help with productivity and increase focused attention. It doesn't have to be much, but gestures like this can transform your meetings.

While most of the suggestions above apply primarily to in-person meetings, you should be intentional about your virtual meeting environments, as well. Whether you're hosting or simply attending a virtual meeting, you want to strive for professionalism. Sure, a pet or a child may interrupt you during a video conference. That happens occasionally in my company, and when it does, we usually laugh it off and roll with it. However, that doesn't mean you shouldn't *try* to avoid these distractions when joining a meeting remotely. For example, you could:

- Select an environment with minimal background noise. Coffee shops probably don't qualify.

- Pick a place with a background that's visually appealing but not too distracting.

- Make sure you have good lighting, especially on your face. Also, beware of lighting behind you, as that can be hard on the eyes of the person you're meeting with.

- Decorate a home office setup with virtual meetings in mind. Turn on your computer's camera and see how much of your office is visible. Then, add a few nice touches within the camera shot.

- Consider hanging a sign on the door to your office to let others know you're in a meeting.

As we've said before, virtual meetings are as much a part of modern business as in-person meetings. If you're leading one or just attending one, you want to make it as attractive, comfortable, and customized to the meeting topic as possible.

EVERYONE PREPARES

Most of the information in this chapter has been designed with the organizer in mind, but the meeting leader isn't the only person who should spend time in preparation before a meeting. Nancy Rothbard rightly argues that *everyone*—leaders and participants—have an obligation to prepare for the meeting. "We're so busy that we just don't prepare," she explains in *Knowledge@ Wharton*, "and when we don't prepare there is a lot of wasted time. And that's incredibly frustrating, because the problem is . . . not across the board. Some people come in super prepared, and those are the people who are most frustrated."

Others, she says, come into the meeting without having spent any time thinking about the problem everyone's gathering to solve. Instead, the unprepared see the meeting itself as the time to think about the issue for the first time. Seriously, this borders on rude. If the meeting was scheduled well in advance, and if the meeting invitation clearly outlined the purpose and scope of the meeting, every attendee should walk in prepared to have a meaningful, informed discussion. Walking in unprepared shows disrespect for the hard work of others who took the meeting request seriously.

"Traditional meetings follow a well-worn groove," says Dana Ardi, a consultant who works with large corporations, in Joanne Cleaver's *Business Researcher* article: "Set a time and agenda; prepare; attend; follow through. Thus, anticipating a meeting forces participants to prepare, clarify their thoughts and validate information . . . . It's a whole value chain that surrounds the meeting."

That value chain matters to everyone in the room. When people show up prepared for a great discussion, everyone wins. The stragglers might feel uncomfortable when everyone else hits the ground running at the start of the meeting. Good. Let that discomfort motivate them to make some changes to their meeting prep. And, if those changes never come, you might identify some team members who are simply taking up space.

Whether you're the organizer or an attendee, a good meeting should impact your calendar at least three times:

- Before: Preparation

- During: The meeting itself

- After: The follow-up, which we'll discuss in Step 5.

That means your hour-long meeting will take up more than an hour of each participant's time. With that in mind, and as you work through your preparation and create the detailed agenda, keep a close eye on the list of participants you invited (per Step 1). If you realize someone's not needed and they haven't already prepared something, you should excuse them from the meeting. My guess is, they won't mind. If you keep them in the meeting, at least make sure they have something to contribute.

Preparation can be time-consuming, and it may not feel natural at first. Do it anyway. Consistency in our preparation has worked wonders in my company's meeting culture. Everyone in the organization knows that our meetings will be well organized and follow the same general pattern.

Because our leaders are trained in this process, our team members trust us not to waste their time in meetings. They know they'll receive a detailed agenda at the start of every meeting, and they know the order of the program, outlined above. Plus, they know their leaders have put some thought into creating the ideal environment for the discussion. As a result, our meetings stay fun, focused, and on point, and they begin and end on time—but only if the meeting leader and facilitator actually *follow* the agenda and lead the meeting well. That's what we'll talk about next.

STEP 4

MEET

Showtime! By the day of the meeting, you have put a lot of time and energy into deciding, scheduling, and planning. Now it's time to put all that effort to work by leading an effective, productive meeting.

That word *productive* is important. Meetings have a reputation for being the most unproductive times of the week for a reason. Employees see meetings as interruptions, as the things that pull them away from their *real* work. The blame for that, I think, falls at the feet of meeting organizers and facilitators who do a terrible job leading the meeting. The fundamental responsibility of the meeting leader is to drive a discussion that leads to an action or decision. If you're not doing that, you're failing as a meeting leader.

But there's hope. You've already invested heavily in the front end of the meeting with your quality preparation. Now you're ready to head into the meeting with four clear goals: to lead the conversation, make effective use of technology, avoid annoying meeting behaviors, and end the meeting with action.

LEAD THE CONVERSATION

If you don't know how to lead a good meeting, you aren't alone. And, to be honest, it's probably not your fault. According to Emily Pidgeon's summary of the research, 75 percent of people have received no formal training on how to conduct a meeting, and yet most leaders are dropped at the head of a conference table and expected to drive a discussion on a regular basis.

We aren't born knowing how to lead a meeting; it's not a genetic trait we get from our parents. It's a skill we must learn. After leading hundreds of good meetings (and suffering through thousands of bad ones), I believe a good conversation comes down to four things:

❶ Staying on topic

❷ Guarding against distractions

❸ Asking good questions

❹ Facilitating transformative conflict

If you can do those four things, you'll be miles ahead of most meeting leaders, so let's break them down a bit.

Staying on topic. A quarter of the meeting time is spent discussing irrelevant issues, according to Pidgeon. In my experience, the time spent chasing rabbits and following tangents is even worse than that. If you've spent any time in meetings, you know exactly what I'm talking about. The discussion is going one way, but someone brings up a *partially* related issue and the conversation starts to go off course. More people chime in with more thoughts on the new topic. Within minutes, everyone flocks around—even argues about—something completely unrelated to the matter at hand. Too often, that type of discussion creep completely takes over a meeting and results in no decisions being made and no action being taken on the key issue.

Every meeting is going to stray off course at times, and it's the meeting leader's job to head it off before it gains momentum. That's why the agenda is vital. The agenda is your roadmap. With rare exception, if a topic isn't on the agenda, it doesn't belong in the meeting. When those side issues pop up, a good meeting leader cuts off the conversation and tables that topic for another time.

If you tell the room you're going to come back to it later, be sure you have a system in place to collect these new ideas. You can call it a back burner, parking lot, follow-up list, whatever you want. Just make a note and be sure to address it at a later time. If the issue deserves its own meeting, do so *later*. There will be time for that, but the time is not in the middle of the present meeting. Have the discipline to shut it down and carry on with your agenda.

Another thing that takes a meeting off track is having too many conversations going on at one time. I struggled with this in meetings until I instituted what my friend Luci Swindoll calls the One Conversation Rule. In any gathering, whether it's a business meeting or family dinner, strive to have only one conversation going at a time. Cut off any side chatter as quickly as possible and redirect everyone's attention back to the main topic; even better, lay that ground rule at the start of the meeting. This keeps everyone's focus where it belongs, and it helps each participant develop genuine listening skills.

In free-for-all conversations, everyone vies for attention by being the most clever, humorous, or snarky. That fractures the discussion. If you listen to the person on your right, you'll miss the joke on your left. The result is that no one is really paying attention to anyone. It's like watching a battle of the bands—every act gets a chance to stand out and be noticed; talent and volume are all that matter. But the One Conversation Rule works more like a symphony—everyone is engaged, sometimes simultaneously. However, by focusing on one conversation, there's a place for each voice, and each voice adds to the total effect.

Guarding against distractions. By distraction, I mean anything that's not directly related to the meeting. The two biggest offenders here are multitasking and, believe it or not, daydreaming.

Multitasking—in this case, doing other work during the meeting—is not only disrespectful, it's a complete waste. When we try to do two things at once, we don't do either of them well. That doesn't stop us from trying, though. Three quarters of employees do other work during meetings, according to Pidgeon. The problem is you can't really focus on two tasks at once. If you read and respond to an email during a meeting, there is almost no chance that you're keeping up with the conversation going on around you. You may perk up when your name or department is mentioned, but then you either have to scramble to make sense of what's being said or you have to ask the person speaking to repeat themselves.

The same is true when we get so bored in a meeting that we escape into daydreaming—something Pidgeon says nine out of ten employees admit doing. Meetings shouldn't have a rewind button. If it's worth your time, it's worth your attention. Whenever you lose a participant behind their laptop or see their eyes glaze over, gently bring them back into the conversation. You might even intentionally ask them a direct question to shock them back into the meeting.

Asking good questions. Early in my career, I thought the secret to success was having all the answers. As I've gotten older, though, I've realized that success is less about having the answers and more about asking the right questions.

In the age of Google, answers are the easy part. You can look up virtually anything and have the answer instantaneously. This only happens, though, when you know how to ask the right questions. That's a skill you'll need to learn if you want to lead effective meetings. To help, here are seven quick tips for asking better questions:

❶ Ask open-ended questions. Yes and no questions won't drive a discussion. Strive to ask questions that require the participants' thought and insight.

❷ Get behind the assumptions. Good conversations require you to get beneath the surface. Ask yourself and others, "What are we assuming in this scenario?" Then peel the layers of the onion until you get to the heart of the matter.

❸ Get both sides of the story. You will save yourself a world of embarrassment if you never make a decision until you're sure you know both sides.

❹ Ask follow-up questions. Oftentimes, you won't get to the real meat of an issue until you go several questions deep.

❺ Get comfortable with "dead air." Avoid the temptation to fill an uncomfortable silence yourself. If you let the silence linger, you'll often be surprised at how much information others will offer.

❻ Help people discover their own insights. One of the best ways to mentor others is to *ask* rather than *tell*. Try to ask thoughtful questions that will help others in the room arrive at meaningful conclusions on their own.

❼ Understand the difference between facts and speculation. Be clear on what you *know* and what you *think* you know. Too many bad decisions have been made based on misunderstandings or incomplete facts. When in doubt, ask the room, "Do we know this to be a fact, or are we assuming something?"

When leading a meeting, don't feel pressured to have all the answers yourself. If you knew everything, you wouldn't have needed to call the meeting. Use good questions to drive the conversation, and you'll get the maximum benefit from the brainpower you've assembled.

Facilitating transformative conflict. Lawrence Wilson on the MH&Co team shares a great perspective on conflict. The two traditional ways to handle conflict between team members are *conflict management*, which assumes conflict is a constant feature of group life and something to keep alive within boundaries, and *conflict resolution*, which sees conflict as an interruption of normal life and a problem to be solved and eliminated as quickly as possible.

These two responses represent the extremes. Larry suggests a third option: *conflict transformation.* This approach sees conflict as an opportunity to strengthen the life of any group. So, when conflict inevitably arises in your meeting, don't immediately feel pressured to shut it down as an interruption or dismiss it as a normal part of life. Use it as an opportunity to bring the opposing parties together by examining the real issues at the heart of the disagreement and guiding them toward a solution that is a win-win.

Controlling the conversation isn't always easy, but it's essential for leading meetings. Commit yourself to growing in these four skills with each and every meeting you lead.

MAKE EFFECTIVE USE OF TECHNOLOGY

Whether you're hosting an in-person or a virtual meeting, you need to make the best possible use of technology. Tech has the ability to enhance our meetings and bring laser focus to the conversation. Used incorrectly, however, technology (and tech glitches) can also bring an otherwise good meeting to a screeching halt. The trick is to figure out exactly what you need and stick to the handful of tools you know and trust.

For in-person meetings, I recommend:

- A great whiteboard. This is essential to my team's collaboration during meetings for sketches, lists, and so on. The trick is capturing your work before you erase. You can go expensive (e.g., Google Jamboard) or inexpensive (just scan your traditional whiteboard with Evernote's Scannable app).

- Accommodations for laptops and tablets. Taking detailed notes, looking up information, and other computer tasks are important in any given meeting. Make sure in-person meeting spaces have plenty of electrical outlets, readily available WiFi, and tables for those who need to sit to type notes and access documents. But a warning: This only works when team members resist tech-based distractions in a meeting. Set expectations accordingly.

- Online video conferencing. Video conferencing gives us two great benefits. First, it gives us the freedom to quickly and easily add an online participant to the meeting at a moment's notice. If we need someone to chime in, they can do so from anywhere. Second, it's an easy way for us to record our meetings, even if we don't have anyone joining online.

For virtual meetings, I recommend:

- A quality video conferencing solution. Zoom, Skype, Google Hangouts, and GoToMeeting are popular options. But none will work well without . . .

- A strong Internet connection. Video conferencing demands high bandwidth and a reliable connection.

- Good AV equipment. If virtual meetings are a key piece of your business, I recommend investing in good cameras, lighting, and microphones. You can get by with your laptop's webcam and a pair of earbuds, but you want the audio and video to be clear; otherwise, your virtual meetings will start to feel like a poor substitute for the "real" thing.

One final note for virtual meetings: Pay attention to your environment and your appearance. Many people think it's okay to log into a virtual meeting like they just rolled out of bed. If that's not how you'd show up for an in-person meeting in the office, it shouldn't be how you appear virtually. *Virtual* does not mean *unprofessional.*

AVOID ANNOYING MEETING BEHAVIORS

For much of my career, I spent more time in meetings than out, and I began to catalog the most annoying meeting behaviors (AMBs) I noticed. None of these AMBs are insurmountable on their own; however, when someone combines three or four in a single meeting, it can test the patience of Job. If you're responsible for leading a good meeting, you've got to be on guard for these ten behaviors—not only in others, but also yourself.

❶ Arriving late

❷ Taking phone calls

❸ Checking email

❹ Engaging in side conversations

❺ Not taking notes

❻ Talking too much

❼ Interrupting others

❽ Not coming prepared

❾ Chasing rabbits

❿ Not speaking up

Every one of these things signal disinterest, even disrespect. If people are sitting in your meeting and committing a few of these AMBs, you cannot count on them to contribute anything meaningful to the conversation. The purpose of the meeting is to have a discussion that leads to action and decisions, and that can't happen when people are mentally checking out to write emails, take phone calls, and make jokes to the person sitting next to them. It may not be comfortable, but you've got to deal with these. It's rarely appropriate to do it in front of everyone else, but you should at least confront the offending party in a one-on-one discussion afterward.

I'll add one more AMB to the list, and this is one we're all guilty of: skipping meetings at the last minute. If you've agreed to join someone's meeting, you've made a commitment to them. It may have been a mistake to accept the invitation in the first place, but that decision has already been made. Deciding to skip on the day of the meeting might be okay once or twice, but making a habit out of it will cost you credibility and put your reputation at risk. Plus, you'd be disrespecting the hard work the meeting organizer and others put into planning and preparing for the meeting. You don't want necessary people to drop out of your meetings at the last minute, so you shouldn't do it to them.

A final word about AMBs: They're just as bad in virtual meetings as they are in person. Actually, they could be worse. In a virtual meeting, the camera is locked onto your face. It is immediately obvious to everyone watching whether or not you're paying attention. It's easy to feel alone and isolated when you're joining a meeting remotely, but never forget the fact that the camera is just a few feet away. If you wouldn't do something with someone staring at your face from two feet away, you shouldn't do it in a virtual meeting.

END WITH ACTION

There are a few things to wrap up at the end of the meeting. Sometimes people linger for chitchat. Sometimes they want to race to the next thing. Regardless, end with a call to action. Any meeting that doesn't is a failure.

In the book *Crucial Conversations,* authors Kerry Patterson, Joseph Grenny, Ron McMillan, and Al Switzler say this should be the very last step that happens in any meeting. They conclude:

> You've engaged in healthy dialogue, filled the pool of meaning, decided how you're going to draw from the pool, and eventually come to some decisions. It's time to do something. Some of the items may have been completely resolved during the discussion, but you may require a person or team to do something. You'll have to make some assignments. . . . Determine *who* does *what* by *when*. Make the deliverables crystal clear.

To achieve this, I recommend having the person who recorded the minutes (more on that in Step 5) read off the action items, being careful to articulate them in this specific format:

First, state each action item with a verb. For example, "Review the Milford contract with the agent," or, "Call Jim and get the latest turnover figures." I also recommend adding action items to the top of the minutes, not the bottom where they often fall. The meeting notes template in the back of the book is designed this way.

Second, specify the deliverable. What exactly do you expect the person completing the action to do? It must be an observable behavior with a specific endpoint, such as a phone call, written report, or a presentation. Assign the deliverable to one—and only one—owner so you know who to blame if no one follows through.

Third, agree on a due date. Get a commitment from the person responsible. Be realistic but put it in writing. This is a commitment, and it should be treated as such. Be deliberate about the final step. This is where you see if your meeting was a success, so make it count.

Leading a meeting isn't difficult, but it does require planning and discipline. And, if you're new to leading meetings or have never learned how to do it, it will require some trial and error as you hone your skills. It's worth it, though. Everyone who attends your high-quality, on-topic, action-oriented meetings will appreciate the effort. Most employees have had very few really good meetings throughout their careers; make it your goal to give them one every single time.

Now, with the meeting itself behind you, there's one final step to bring everything to a close: the follow-up. We'll cover that next.

STEP 5

FOLLOW UP

The meeting is finished. But even though the group has dispersed, you still have a few elements to take care of before you can completely put the meeting to bed. Specifically, you need to consider meeting feedback, review your meeting notes, and schedule time to complete your action items (and check on others' action items).

CONSIDER MEETING FEEDBACK

If you want to grow as a meeting leader and continually improve your skills in driving meaningful, action-oriented conversations, you're going to need some thick skin. We've said before that nobody is born knowing how to lead good meetings. It's a skill, and that skill is honed through trial, error, and plenty of practice. You may think you're getting better, but if others don't see it, you're deluding yourself. The only way to know for sure if your meetings are hitting the mark is to consider the feedback you get from those who attend. Your meeting participants give you that crucial feedback in three ways:

❶ What they *say*

❷ How they *act*

❸ What they *do*

This feedback is always coming in; you just have to know how to find it.

First, the most direct way to get feedback is to ask for it. Fair warning, though: This will likely provide mixed results. If the team members are a little lower on the ladder than you are, they may be hesitant to provide criticisms, regardless of the accuracy of their assessment. They may blow smoke and tell you how wonderful and engaging your meetings are—even if they struggled to stay awake the entire time. This could also be true of peers who simply don't want to hurt your feelings. On the other end of the spectrum, you may have a competitive team member in the meeting who exaggerates your flaws in some weird attempt to undermine your leadership. Unfortunate, but it happens.

Your best bet when asking for feedback is to target one or two people whom you know well and trust to give honest feedback. Your direct boss could be a great fit for this, even if they aren't specifically needed in the meeting. As part of your leadership development, you could ask your manager to attend a few of your meetings and provide critical feedback on what you're doing well and what still needs work. Just be ready for honest evaluations. If you don't want to hear criticisms, don't ask for feedback.

Second, watch your meeting participants' body language during the meeting. The people in the room are always giving you feedback. How they act, how often they shift in their seats, whether they're yawning, how well they're engaging in the conversation, how often they're multitasking—all these things tell you if you're running a good or bad meeting.

One bored employee for the Ohio Department of Transportation, for example, turned his meeting drudgery into social media fun. He was constantly stuck in two-hour meetings, but he was only needed for fifteen minutes in the middle. So, he filled the rest of the time doodling superheroes, which he later posted online with the hashtag #meetingfromhell. While that is amusing (unless you were running the meeting), doodling is the kind of feedback meeting participants give us all the time, according to organizational psychology professor Steven Rogelberg. "You're basically getting tremendous amounts of feedback," he said in Yuki Noguchi's report for NPR. "You're getting feedback that you're running a really bad meeting."

Third—and perhaps the best way to measure your effectiveness as a meeting leader—is to evaluate how well the people in the meeting follow through with their action items. Do people complete the tasks they're assigned? Are those tasks driving your business forward? Are real problems being solved? Remember, the whole purpose of the meeting is to drive a discussion that leads to action and decisions. If those actions and decisions aren't making an impact, there's been a breakdown in the process. Either the meeting wasn't really needed—or you didn't run it well.

Feedback isn't always comfortable, but it generally tells you what you need to know. Go into it honestly, and don't be scared to make some changes based on what you discover. After all, this entire book should cause you to make some serious changes to your meeting process. You probably won't get it perfect right off the bat, and, even when you work the process, you'll still find yourself stuck in bad meetings from time to time. Just face it, critically examine where the breakdown was, and make changes to the process for next time. There's no point considering feedback unless you're willing to use those insights to make your future meetings better.

REVIEW MEETING NOTES

If you spend much time in meetings or presentations, note-taking is a survival skill. I've assumed up to this point that you're taking notes in meetings—both the ones you lead and the ones you simply participate in. At the very least, one person should be assigned the task of recording the minutes—even if there are only two people in the meeting. Don't be misled by the term "minutes," as if you have to keep a minute-by-minute detailed log of what each person said. This is usually (in fact, almost always) unnecessary.

In most meetings, recording the key decisions and action items is sufficient. You want to document decisions so there is no misunderstanding later. You also want to document action items so you can hold people accountable and track progress. Beyond that, you're probably just engaging in busywork. Distribute minutes as soon after the meeting as possible so the participants can review the key items while they're fresh in their memory, as well as be reminded of what is expected of them.

Taking minutes is the minimum note-taking required in any given meeting, but I suggest going further and taking personal meeting notes throughout the discussion. This helps you stay engaged, which is especially important for meetings you're not personally leading. It also enables you to capture in-the-moment insights, questions, and commitments. Not everything can be resolved immediately; it's good to have a written record of your (and others') key thoughts so you can go right back to the heart of the matter later, when you're reviewing your notes and taking care of your action items.

Actively taking notes also communicates to the other attendees that you're engaged in the conversation and aren't daydreaming or distracted. And, if you're in leadership, taking notes subtly establishes accountability. Your people will think, *If the boss is writing it down, he probably intends to follow-up. I better pay attention.*

Those are all great benefits to note-taking, but my favorite is the fact that written notes create your own personal time machine. I can't tell you how many times my notes have saved my bacon—not only when trying to resolve a dispute, but also in holding people accountable or retrieving a meaningful insight I subsequently forgot. As important as meeting notes are, though, I don't recall anyone ever teaching me *how* to take notes. Even as a student, no one showed me the best practices for note-taking. I guess we assume people know how to take notes. Sadly, many don't. If that's you, then here are my five ways to create your personal time machine:

First, choose the right tool. Use whatever works best for you, whether it's an app on your computer or tablet or something as basic as a yellow pad. If you don't already have a tool in place, feel free to experiment. Some people prefer to type everything, while others find the physical act of writing by hand helps cement the details in their brains. Find what works for you, and then stick with it.

Second, give your notes structure. Use headers, order, and hierarchy in your notes. Even if the presentation is unstructured, try to add some structure through numbered sections and nested bullets. This will help later when you review your notes.

Third, record whatever is important or interesting. Again, you don't need to capture every word. I suggest focusing on the presenter's outline, questions being asked or answered, key insights, and any useful stories or diagrams that help bring the material to life.

Fourth, use symbols. I indent my notes about a half-inch from the left side of the page. This gives me room to add key symbols beside my notes as needed. I typically use four symbols: a star for something important, a question mark for anything that requires further research, an open square for something that requires my personal follow-up, and an open circle for a follow-up item that's been assigned to someone else. I also include the assignee's initials for those items so I know who's responsible for them.

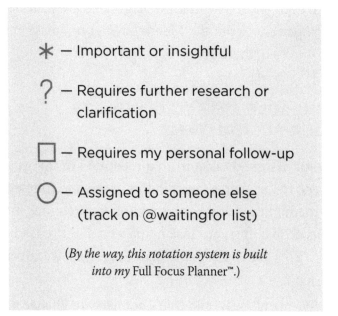

✳ — Important or insightful

? — Requires further research or clarification

☐ — Requires my personal follow-up

○ — Assigned to someone else (track on @waitingfor list)

(By the way, this notation system is built into my Full Focus Planner™.)

Fifth, schedule time to review your notes. This is *key*. I scan my notes immediately after the meeting, if possible. If I can't do it right then, I do it at the end of my workday. On the rare weeks when I miss several days of reviewing meeting notes, I make it part of my weekly review at the end of the week. The danger there, though, is that I may have already missed the opportunity to follow up with people about their assigned tasks. Also, I risk putting my own assigned tasks in jeopardy if I don't quickly review my notes and make sure I've put my action items on my task list or calendar.

Bottom line: No one can count on total, perfect recall. Great notes are the closest thing to a time machine we'll ever get, so use them well. To help get your notes on paper, check out the Meeting Notes template in the Resources of this book.

SCHEDULE TIME TO COMPLETE YOUR ACTION ITEMS

If your assigned tasks from a meeting are things you can do in less than a few minutes, discipline yourself to do them immediately. For anything that requires more time, drop it into your task manager and put a deadline on it. This goes back to the Back Stage time we covered in Step 2.

We are all busy, and that's not likely to change anytime soon. However, you can't be *so* busy that you're unable to complete the tasks that come out of your meetings. That's one reason Back Stage time is so important. For example, even though I know I'll spend most of my Mondays and Fridays in meetings, I still block off time on my schedule on those days to review my meeting notes and make sure I've accounted for the tasks that were assigned to me.

When I know a task will require a block of time, I take the additional step of scheduling a meeting with myself on my calendar to work on it during one of my Back Stage days. By putting it on my calendar, I know I'm securing enough time to get the work done and I'm holding myself accountable to the due date I agreed to. With the task on my calendar, I can forget about it for awhile without worrying that I'll lose track of it or let others down.

Your personal action items aren't the only ones you need to track, though. If you led the meeting, you're ultimately responsible for the outcome—even the tasks that weren't assigned to you. The meeting should produce meaningful decisions and actions; if it doesn't, no matter who dropped the ball, it's on you. That means you need to create a system for following up on others' action items, and you need to hold them accountable for following through. After the meeting, I recommend simply creating an additional task for yourself called

"Follow Up with Everyone Else's Tasks."

Set aside a few minutes at an appropriate time to check in on the responsible team members and to ask if they have any other questions about what's expected of them. You can do this through additional one-on-one check-in meetings, or, better yet, quick notes by email, Slack, or through your project management system. Do *enough* to let them know their task is still on your radar, but not *so much* that you come across as a micromanager. Nobody needs or wants that.

FIX OR QUIT

That's it. Those are the five steps to ensuring every single one of your meetings gets the results you want. That's how you keep the conversation on point, keep everyone engaged, make crucial decisions, hold people accountable, and drive genuine change in your organization.

There are far too many failed meetings taking place all over the country right now, at this very moment. It's time to make yourself the exception. Give your meetings the no fail guarantee by following the five steps:

1. Decide

2. Schedule

3. Prepare

4. Meet

5. Follow Up

It's time to redeem your meetings. Believe it or not, good meetings—the best meetings—are totally worth the effort. As much as we sometimes hate them, meetings have tremendous power to move our projects and priorities forward. How well we organize and run our meetings can also be the best way to judge a company's effectiveness and organizational health.

Meetings don't have to be pointless, painful, and all consuming. They're meant to be selectively scheduled and consistently productive. And now you know how to engineer that outcome. If you follow the five steps, you'll not only breathe new life into your meetings, you'll experience dramatic changes throughout your entire organization.

Your team deserves it, and so do you. But let me tell you what you and your team don't deserve: to continue the status quo. So, I want to close out *No-Fail Meetings* by helping you quit at least some of the meetings you can't fix.

PERMISSION TO SAY NO

Even if a meeting is needed, there's a good chance *you're not*. Maybe you like having a hand in everything, but that kind of personal investment isn't sustainable, especially as you take on new responsibilities or move up in an organization. "The more successful you become," says Andy Stanley, "the less accessible you will be." As we become successful, we face greater demands on our time and resources. We can't give everything or everyone the same level of attention and the same amount of time we once did; there just aren't enough hours in our increasingly busy days. And so, we must do what many of us hate: say no.

I don't have enough room in this book to convince you of the need for, freedom in, and the power of saying the little word *no*. If you, like me, have struggled with this, you'd be amazed at how life-transforming this one-syllable miracle-worker can be. However, if I've at least convinced you that your time might be better spent outside of the meetings that are dragging you down, let me offer five quick tips for taking your time back from the meeting monster:

First, cancel standing meetings that no longer add value. Nobody likes to waste time. Your team will thank you for canceling a meeting that's wasting theirs.

Second, challenge meetings that others have scheduled. Share this book and its principles with others in your organization so you can all get better at deciding if a meeting is necessary. At the least, you may need to re-train others on how to send quality, informative meeting invitations.

Third, consider or suggest alternatives to meeting. People don't *have* to meet to have a discussion. Maximize other communication methods, such as email, Slack, and your project management systems. You'd be surprised what you can accomplish outside of meetings. One form I created years ago is the Recommended Briefing Form. For any initiative under consideration, you can provide a recommendation, the background details, the rationale for your recommendation, plus a timetable and financial impact, including anticipated cost, potential upside, and so on. (I've included an RBF in the resources section in the back.) All of that can happen outside a meeting, saving the discussion for email or Slack. Or it can cut the meeting time in half by clearly defining the parameters of the conversation, which leads me to the next tip.

Fourth, cut or recommend cutting the length of meetings. As we saw in Step 2, meetings will almost always take up the full time allotted. Make the meeting time shorter and you'll probably get the same amount of work done.

Fifth, stop attending low-leverage meetings. Your time is valuable. If you don't think you have anything to add to the discussion, ask to be excused. Or, if it's within your power, excuse yourself!

The only way to take your time back from bad, irrelevant meetings is to flex your *no* muscle. The good news is that it gets easier the more you do it, especially once you start reaping the rewards of recovered time.

THE GREAT ESCAPE

If you're not an entrepreneur or C-level executive, you probably have to attend meetings your boss or other leaders have scheduled. You also may not have the power to simply abolish any meeting that seems unnecessary. The key to your productivity, though, is setting boundaries that protect your time for optimal focus. Believe it not, you have the autonomy to do this to some degree, regardless of your role in the company. Rather than seeing yourself as a victim of a meeting-heavy, distraction-filled organization, try to make a break for it.

There are ways to escape pointless meetings, but it'll require some creativity. First, strategically assess all the meetings on your plate and decide which one(s) could get by without you and from which you'd reclaim the most time if you could skip. Next, ask your boss or the meeting organizer if you can sit it out. When you do, be sure to anticipate and answer the one question they're already asking themselves: *What's in it for me?* That is, if you can demonstrate that your time will be better used elsewhere—in a way that directly benefits *their* interests—you'll likely have a winning case.

Here are three message examples to get you started. You can copy and modify these however you need.

Sally,

I wanted to make a quick request regarding the interdepartmental weekly budget review meeting on Fridays.
I'd like to ask for permission to excuse

myself from that meeting, or at the very least, attend only the last week of each month. My role in that meeting is minimal, and the information shared does not directly relate to the success of my position.

As you know, I am really committed to the growth of our department and want to do excellent work. It's become increasingly tough, though, to find time on my calendar to accomplish it well. I believe that reclaiming those two hours a week will be just what I need to finish our team's sales reports with more care—and get them to you earlier in the day. That extra time will offer you ample time to review, as well, without the normal rush that often keeps us here late Friday evening.

I know the completion of the sales reports is critical, and I'd love to make that my priority on Fridays. I think that using the budget review meeting time to complete the reports more thoroughly will be a huge win-win for all.

I'll be sure to get the meeting minutes from Carol each week and review them carefully.

Best,
David

Hi Mrs. Jones,

I'd like to suggest that I no longer be included in the monthly production meetings, and here's why:

That meeting falls the day before my monthly design mockups are due to our client, and it's a tough interruption to my focus time. Using those 90 minutes to complete the assets would allow me to do so with less rush and more excellence—plus, I'd be able to share them with the team for review earlier in the day.

Since my role in the monthly production meeting is minimal and I can easily get the information later from Russell, I believe it would be a win-win for the entire team if I were allowed to give my full attention to those client assets.

I'm fully committed to our team and truly appreciate the proactive nature with which you share information, but I am confident this change will give you peace of mind and review time, plus the client will receive materials more quickly each week.

Thanks for considering!
Julie

Hey Adam,

Suzanne in marketing here. I wanted to run something by you. If possible, I'd like to sit out of the Monday morning sales update meetings. I'd love to, instead, use that time to pull together the weekend sales data report. Monday mornings are the best time for doing so, and being excused from the meeting would allow me to get that data to you before lunchtime. I know that would be awesome for you, as you often meet with retailers around noon. Just a thought! It would be a win-win for us both, and I'd be sure I stay up to speed by getting the meeting minutes from my assistant.

Thanks, Adam!
Suzanne

IT'S UP TO YOU

What if you revolutionized how your organization does meetings and redeemed the hundreds of hours your company may be losing to bad meetings every year? What if you freed your team members from meetings they don't need to be in and gave them back the time they needed for their high-leverage work? This may be as simple as asking one key question: *Do we really need to meet about this?* If the answer is no, congratulations! You just redeemed some lost time. But if the answer is yes, make the absolute best use of everyone's time.

People want to feel effective and connected at work. Meetings give them that opportunity, but only if they're well led. Meetings give you the chance to take your organization to new heights or bring it crashing down in an avalanche of mediocrity and misery.

If you're calling, leading, or participating in meetings, guess what? The difference between a good meeting and a bad meeting is *you*. So, kill or quit the meetings that aren't needed—and revolutionize the ones that are.

EXTRA RESOURCES

ROUTINE MEETINGS

Different organizations and teams will have different kinds of routine meetings. Some of them are critical; many are not. Use the list below as inspiration for meetings you might need to add and to target ones you could eliminate.

DAILY

EXECUTIVE ASSISTANT CHECK-IN

- *Suggested length*: 10–20 minutes

- *Description*: Short, daily update and organization huddle between an executive and his/her assistant. Usually best at the start and/or end of the day. Could be a daily or weekly routine.

WEEKLY

THE COMPANY-WIDE TEAM HUDDLE

- *Suggested length*: 30–60 minutes, depending on meeting scope

- *Description*: Company-wide meeting at the start of every week. Includes a review of company goals, financial updates, and each department's big wins from the previous week and priorities for the week ahead.

DEPARTMENT HUDDLE

- *Suggested length*: 30–60 minutes

- *Description*: Department-level meeting where the department's quarterly goals are shared and progress updates are given. The department's top priorities for the week are restated and each team member is given time to share wins, priorities, and questions.

DIRECT REPORT ONE-ON-ONE

- *Suggested length*: 15–30 minutes for non-leadership roles; up to an hour for executive and leadership roles

- *Description*: Regular opportunity for leaders to meet individually with their direct reports. Leaders of larger teams may prefer to do this monthly.

MONTHLY

EXECUTIVE TEAM FINANCIAL AND GOAL REVIEW

- *Suggested length*: 4–6 hours

- *Description*: Executive Team reviews the previous month's financial reports and annual/ quarterly goals, shares progress updates, and discusses the coming month/quarter to calibrate priorities. Often includes time for leaders to work together to discuss solutions for a problem or to brainstorm new ideas.

PRINCIPALS IDEATION DAY

- *Suggested length*: Full day

- *Description*: All-day meeting for the principals of the company (such as the CEO and COO) to collaborate. Agenda includes specific challenges that need resolutions and decisions that need to be made. Unstructured time is also given for brainstorming and long-term vision casting. Main idea is to create space for top-level leaders to rise above the day-to-day demands and focus strategically on the future of the business.

LEADERSHIP TEAM MEETING

- *Suggested length*: 1–2 hours, depending on the size of the team

- *Description*: Brings all leaders across the company together as one leadership team. Each leader is given time to share their recent wins and challenges. Time is given for troubleshooting key issues in others' departments. Often includes time for leadership development and/or group book studies. Held in an intimate location, such as a leader's home over breakfast.

QUARTERLY

TEAM TRAINING AND GOAL SETTING

- *Suggested length*: Full day

- *Description*: Time for the entire team—including remote employees—to come together in person to focus on three key goals: development, connection, and quarterly goal-setting. May include professional development by a key executive or outside speaker. Time is given for company-wide goal updates before everyone breaks up by department to review and set departmental quarterly goals. This all-day meeting also includes time for fun and team building, and it is best held offsite.

QUARTERLY REVIEW

- *Suggested length*: All day for business owners; half day for executives; two hours for staff

- *Description*: Dedicated to quarterly goal reviews and previews. Includes time to reflect on:

  - *Biggest Wins*: Outline your biggest accom-
    plishments for the quarter.

  - *After-Action Review*: Identify what worked/
    didn't work with your goals for the past
    quarter.

  - *Annual Goal Review*: Review your current
    list of annual goals. Revise, update, remove,
    or replace as needed. Identify which quar-
    ter you plan to work on each goal.

  - *Monthly Calendar Review*: Look at the
    year as a whole and identify your main
    focus for each month. Be sure to update
    your calendar with each month's major
    events, major deadlines, major projects,
    and rejuvenation (rest/play) time.

ANNUALLY

TEAM RETREAT

- *Suggested length*: 3–5 days

- *Description*: Off-site retreat for the entire team.
  Especially effective for bringing remote team
  members together. Emphasis should be on fun

and team building, but it should also include a few structured meetings for company-wide updates, announcements, and new initiatives. Best scheduled near the transition to a new fiscal year to rally the team around the organization's key strategic goals. This can/should be as fun and extravagant as appropriate for the organization. Examples include mountain retreat centers or company cruises.

EXECUTIVE STRATEGIC PLANNING

- *Suggested length*: 2–3 days

- *Description:* Annual meeting of the executive team devoted to reviewing the previous year's goals and formulating the coming year's goals. Each day has a focus. A sample three-day agenda may look like this:

  - *Day 1, Review and Reflect*: Review the company values, mission, hiring updates, financial overview, and wins/losses on the previous year's goals.

  - *Day 2, Brainstorming*: All-day creative thinking around the organization's future.

  - *Day 3, Projection and Goals*: Draft the coming year's new goals, project revenue, create a general draft of the budget, and plan for new hires.

ANNUAL EMPLOYEE REVIEWS

- *Suggested length*: 1–2 hours

- *Description*: Opportunity for leaders to meet with each employee on their work anniversary. Time is spent celebrating the team member's successes, honestly reviewing their challenges and problem areas, and evaluating their general performance for the year. Success is measured by the team member's job description, key results areas, personal/team goals, and other agreed-upon metrics. The discussion should be open and honest but should maintain a fun, celebratory atmosphere as appropriate.

MEETING NOTES

MEETING INFORMATION

MEETING TITLE	
DATE & TIME	
PARTICIPANTS	
MEETING LEADER	
MEETING FACILITATOR	
LINK TO AGENDA	

TABLED ITEMS TO DISCUSS LATER

DISCUSSION ITEM	WHO SHOULD OWN FOLLOW UP ON THIS ITEM?

ACTIVATE OWNERSHIP

ACTION ITEM	OWNER & TARGET COMPLETION DATE

GENERAL NOTES

MEETING AGENDA

MEETING INFORMATION

MEETING TITLE	
DATE & TIME	
PARTICIPANTS	
MEETING LEADER	
MEETING FACILITATOR	

MEETING PURPOSE

PRIMARY PURPOSE	
DESIRED RESULTS	

MEETING PROGRAM

TIME ALLOCATED	DISCUSSION ITEM	NOTES & RESOURCES
	Celebrate Achievements	
	Celebrate Expectations	

continued on next page

TIME ALLOCATED	DISCUSSION ITEM	NOTES & RESOURCES
	Meeting Content *(build this around your desired results and purpose)*	
	Meeting Content *(build this around your desired results and purpose)*	
	Meeting Content *(build this around your desired results and purpose)*	
	Activate Ownership	

RECOMMENDATION BRIEFING FORM

Include Date

RECOMMENDATION

I am recommending that...

[SUMMARIZE WHAT YOU ARE RECOMMENDING.]

BACKGROUND

[PROVIDE A ONE PARAGRAPH SUMMARY OF THE BACKGROUND FOR YOUR RECOMMENDATION.]

RATIONALE

[PROVIDE THE REASONS WHY YOU ARE MAKING THIS RECOMMENDATION.]

TIMETABLE

[PROVIDE THE TIMETABLE FOR THIS
RECOMMENDATION.]

FINANCIAL IMPACT

[PLEASE PROVIDE THE FINANCIAL CONTEXT NEEDED
FOR ME TO MAKE THIS DECISION.]

1. What is the anticipated cost?

2. What is the ROI projection that justifies this? If
   it is just an increased cost, please indicate how
   this happened.

3. What did we originally have in the budget, and
   what were the assumptions there?

4. How does this impact the NOI Forecast positively
   or negatively? Please provide specific numbers.
   And, please bullet your assumptions for those
   projections below.

Download copies at NoFailMeetings.com/resources

SOURCES

- Christopher Bergland, "Exposure to Natural Light Improves Workplace Performance," *Psychology Today*, 5 June 2013, https://www.psychologytoday.com/us/blog/the-athletes-way/201306/exposure-natural-light-improves-workplace-performance.

- "Clarizen Survey: Workers Consider Status Meetings a Productivity-Killing Waste of Time," Clarizen, 6 February 2015, http://www.clarizen.com/about-us/press-releases/item/clarizen-survey-workers-consider-status-meetings-a-productivity-killing-waste-of-time.html.

- Joanne Cleaver, "Meetings and Team Management," *Business Researcher*, 14 March 2016, http://businessresearcher.sagepub.com/sbr-1775-99376-2723046/20160314/meetings-and-team-management.

- Bob Ford, "Harnessing the Power of Natural Light," *Workplace Design*, 24 May 2017, https://workdesign.com/2017/05/harnessing-power-natural-light.

- Jason Fried and David Heinemeier Hansson, *Rework* (Crown Business, 2010).

- David Grady, "How to Save the World (Or At Least Yourself) from Bad Meetings," TED.com, October 2013, https://www.ted.com/talks/david_grady_how_to_save_the_world_or_at_least_yourself_from_bad_meetings.

- Kevan Lee, "9 Science-Backed Methods for More Productive Meetings," *Fast Company*, 21 July 2014, https://www.fastcompany.com/3033232/9-science-backed-methods-for-more-productive-meetings.

- Michael Mankins, "This Weekly Meeting Took Up 300,000 Hours a Year," *Harvard Business Review*, 29 April 2014, https://hbr.org/2014/04/how-a-weekly-meeting-took-up-300000-hours-a-year.

- "Meetings: The Good, the Bad and the Ugly," *Knowledge@Wharton*, 16 September 2015, http://knowledge.wharton.upenn.edu/article/meetings-the-good-the-bad-and-the-ugly.

- Yuki Noguchi, "And So We Meet, Again: Why The Workday Is So Filled With Meetings," NPR, 29 January 2015, https://www.npr.org/2015/01/29/382162271/and-so-we-meet-again-why-the-workday-is-so-filled-with-meetings.

- Kerry Patterson et al., *Crucial Conversations* (McGraw-Hill, 2012).

- Emily Pidgeon, "The Economic Impact of Bad Meetings," TED.com, 17 November 2014, https://ideas.ted.com/the-economic-impact-of-bad-meetings.

- Seneca, *Dialogues and Letters*, trans. C.D.N. Costa (Penguin, 1997).

- Lawrence W. Wilson, "6 Ways to Transform Conflict," MichaelHyatt.com, 15 December 2012, https://michaelhyatt.com/6-ways-to-transform-conflict.

- Matt Woodley, "Catalyst 2011 Andy Stanley: Be Present," *Christianity Today*, October 2011, http://www.christianitytoday.com/pastors/2011/october-online-only/catalyst-2011-andy-stanley-be-present.html.

PLAN YOUR YEAR, DESIGN YOUR DAYS, AND ACHIEVE YOUR BIGGEST GOALS.

FULL
F◎CUS
PLANNER

Michael Hyatt's signature paper planner is the perfect priority-based solution for high achievers seeking an intentional, fulfilling lifestyle.

- Offers tactical solutions to act on your highest priorities, both day-to-day and year-to-year.
- Designed to keep your priorities in clear view, so that you set your course, stay on track, and achieve what matters every day.
- Crafted with sewn binding, ribbon markers, high-quality paper, and clutter-free design — the perfect combination of elegance and function.

Aesthetically pleasing, thoughtfully crafted, uniquely effective.

FULLFOCUSPLANNER.COM